# 101 *Secret* Way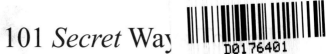
# If You Are Living You~~r Life~~ Purpose!

Daniel Ortiz

First Edition

Infinity Publishing, Inc.

# 101 Secret Ways To Tell If You Are Living Your Life Purpose!

By Daniel Ortiz

Published by:     **Infinity Publishing, Inc.**
**P.O. Box 1784**
**Santa Fe, NM 87504**

Printed and bound in the United States of America

*Man has come here with a definite purpose.*
*Life is not meant merely for eating, drinking*
*and procreating.*

*- Sivanda*

*The purpose of life is to acquaint man with*
*himself.*

*- Ralph Waldo Emmerson*

*The peace of God is my one goal; the aim*
*of all my living here, the end I seek, my*
*purpose and my function and my life, while*
*I abide where I am not at home.*

*- A Course In Miracles*

*There is no road to success but through a*
*clear strong purpose. Nothing can take its*
*place....A purpose is the eternal condition*
*of success.*

*- Theodore Munger*

*Strange is our situation upon earth. Each of*
*us comes for a short visit, not knowing why,*
*yet sometimes seeming to a divine purpose.*

*- Albert Einstein*

*The only true happiness comes from*
*squandering ourselves for a purpose.*

*- William Cowper (1731-1800)*

*Purpose is what gives life meaning.*

*- C.H. Parkhusrt*

*Life without purpose is a languid, drifting*
*thing; every day we ought to review our*
*purpose, saying to ourselves: This day let*
*me make a sound beginning, for what we*
*have hitherto done is naught! Our*
*improvement is in proportion to our*
*purpose.*

*- Thomas A. Kempis*

*Strong lives are motivated by dynamic*
*purposes.*

*- Kenneth Hildebrand*

*I think the purpose of life is to be useful, to*
*be responsible, to be honorable, to be*
*compassionate. It is after all, to matter; to*
*count, to stand for something, to have*
*made some difference that you lived at all.*

*- Leo C. Rosten*

*True happiness...is not attained through*
*self-gratification, but through fidelity to a*
*worthy purpose.*

*- Helen Keller*

*The human heart refuses to believe in a*
*universe without purpose.*

*- Immanuel Kant*

*All we have to do, the Beings told me, is*
*view ourselves as spiritual beings, living*
*in a spiritual place, with a spiritual*
*purpose.*

*- Danion Brinkley-Saved By The Light*

*May He grant you according to your hearts*
*desire, and fulfill all your purpose.*

*- Psalm 20:4*

*The purpose of life is a life purpose.*

*- Robert Byrne*

*When I was going through my transition*
*of being famous, I tried to ask God why*
*I was here? What was my purpose. Surely it*
*wasn't just to win three gold medals. There*
*has to be more to life than that.*

*- Wilma Rudolph (1940-1994)*
*U.S. Olympic Track Team*

*The great and glorious masterpiece of man*
*is to know how to live to purpose.*

*- Washington Iriving*

*To have no set purpose in one's life is the*
*harlotry of the will.*

*- Stephen McKenna*

*There is no such thing as perfection...and*
*our purpose for living is to find that*
*perfection and show it forth.*

*- Richard Bach*

*Many flounder about life because*
*they have no purpose. Before it is*
*possible to achieve anything, an*
*objective must be set.*

*- George Halas (1835-1983)*

*Clear purpose is half the struggle.*

*- Savakram*

*A man without a purpose is like a ship*
*without a rudder...Have a purpose in life,*
*and having it, throw into your work such*
*strength of mind and muscle as God has*
*given you.*

*- Thomas Carlyle*

*The purpose of man's life is not happiness,*
*but worthiness.*

*- Felix Adler*

Lois McCrew!

Karen
Merry
Christmas
from
2019

# _Dedication_

_I want to dedicate this book to the following people
without whom this book would never have been possible._

To my parents Eloy & Fabiola:
Who never lost faith in me.
To my Dad who taught me by example the love of work
that is purposeful. To my Mom who never fails to cook me
enchiladas, beans & chile when I come home.

To my sisters Kathy & Patricia:
Who put up with me while we were growing up.
I am very proud of you both.

To my niece Rachel & nephew Michael:
Who remind me of what is really important in life.
You bring us all so much joy!

To the other members of my extended family who have put their
faith and trust in me by investing in Infinity:
Donald & Cecilia Sanchez, Herman & Rosina Tapia,
& Richard & Cathy Lucero. Thank you for believing in me.

To my grandparents who have passed on to a higher realm but left me
the greatest of inheritances - their love, my memories & our family.

Pablo Dean (1902-1971)
Juanita Dean (1903-1983)
Valentino Ortiz (1910-1991)
Eva Ortiz (1916-1995)

# *Acknowledgements*

*I want to thank the following people whose lives have influenced and inspired the creation of this book.*

Beth Harding:
Who's letter started the process that led to the creation of this book.
The time we spent together was truly magical.

My Unit Managers and Co-workers at Citibank.
Who remind me that the Higher Purpose of our jobs
is not the money we earn but the relationships we make.

Michele Grasso:
Who's input and editing made this book possible.
This book is part of you.

Judy Irving:
Who helped me "bridge the gap" on more than one occasion.
You are proof that angels walk the earth.

Robert Borovay:
Who's help during the "rough times" made my life easier.

Michele Kennedy:
Who taught me that true love need not possess.
You made me feel Alive!

To All who have heard *"The Call"* and answered.
Your Light has shown us The Way!

To all of you who seek your Divine Purpose.
Thank you for helping me fulfill mine.

# Preface

Whoever you are, if you are reading these words, at this particular moment in time, I have a message meant specifically for you. It is a simple message really, and very old. I am neither its source nor am I the first, or the last, to deliver it. You may have heard it before, for it has been expressed in many, many ways. This book is simply my chosen method of expression.

There is no such thing as coincidence. There is a purpose for everything. If you are reading this book now it is because you have come to that stage in life when you may be asking yourself, maybe unconsciously, man's perennial questions:

Who am I?
Why am I here?
What is the purpose of my life?

My message to you is: *You were born for a purpose. You have a mission in this life!*

I first began to ask these questions about 10 years ago while in my late twenties. I was struggling to rebuild my financial planning practice after the stock market crash of 1987 had devastated Wall Street and therefore my securities business. I felt like fate had dealt me a bad hand. My prior success in business was replaced with frustration, disappointment and anger as I struggled to regain the commission income lost as a result of the dramatic plunge in the stock market. Nothing in my life seemed to go right after that day. I began to think that something was wrong with me. I started to question my values, beliefs and very existence. It was then that I began to sincerely search for the meaning of life and for a purpose greater than my own financial security. I decided to surrender my life to a Higher Power.

In hindsight, that experience was a major, and I can now say, necessary step in my personal and spiritual growth. Although I could not discern it at the time, the struggles and frustration I endured served a purpose. I was forced to look *inside* myself for the first time in my life. I recognized that I needed to elevate my level of thinking beyond the limits of the five senses. That is when I discovered a great secret.

Since recorded history, sages, poets and prophets from all cultures and religions have reminded us to look *within* and discover the treasure hidden there. And to seek, as the bible tells us, is to find. It was at that time that I began to have what I can only describe as "mystical" experiences.

These experiences showed me that there is more to life than the accumulation of material wealth or the satisfaction of, what are ultimately, insatiable desires. Neither is life meant to be about enduring suffering or proving we are "good" in order to be rewarded in some afterlife. Nor are we born simply to reproduce and thereby propagate the species ad infinitum. No, the purpose of life is so much simpler and rewarding and is found in the here and now!

I also discovered that I was not alone in my search. Who has never gazed up at the stars at night, beheld that great and magnificent scene and wondered if there was a Divine Plan? And if there was such a Plan, their purpose in it? All ancient wisdom books contain stories about man's quest for Truth.

Most of us don't grow up thinking about a specific purpose in life. Nor do we live our lives in the context of a Divine Plan. Such concepts have been delegated to religion and philosophy. Our paradigm for living is a linear scale somewhere between the extremes of physical and economic survival and financial and professional "success." The assumption is that once we reach a certain level of achievement, we will naturally be happy. Nirvana, we are led to believe, is found when we have "made it."

However, even a casual observation of the personal lives of the rich and famous reveals a different reality. The list of suicides, divorces, and drug and alcohol addiction among this group is too long and too tragic to mention. I do not mean to imply that striving for personal and professional achievement is inherently futile. To the contrary, I believe that a fully actualized individual will, *as a consequence of fulfilling a higher purpose,* reach the heights of success in their chosen field. My message is simply that wealth, fame and power, the things our society teaches us to pursue, *in and of themselves,* do not make us happy. These aspirations must be connected to something greater than oneself in order to derive any sense of lasting satisfaction and peace of mind.

I first came to this realization in 1995 on a beautiful summer evening while cruising up the Nile River in Egypt. I had just arrived from Spain. You see, until that moment, I believed my purpose in life was to travel the world, experience new and exotic places and meet interesting people. Living what we Latins call, *"La Dolce Vita."* Although I was enjoying my discoveries, I had to admit to myself that *something* was still missing. I asked myself the same question many ask after fulfilling their life's ambitions; *"Is this all there is?"*

At that moment, I got *"The Message!"* It was like getting hit with a velvet hammer; gentle, yet very strong. It came from that still small Voice we all have inside us. I am not referring to intuition or gut instinct. No, this is an actual Voice that comes directly from our spiritual Source. Each of us can hear this Voice. Not all of us have learned to listen and trust what it says.

The Voice conveyed my true purpose and revealed what was missing from my life. In a moment of revelation, I finally understood why we would never feel complete, satisfied or content if we live only for ourselves. Our Life Purpose is a *paradox*. It is not just about us - and it is just about us. The reason is that we are all connected to one another - *spiritually*. When we help others we also help ourselves. Serving humanity is our purpose. Extending love is the means. The healing of our soul is the result.

How do we accomplish this?

Every one of us has been endowed with a special gift, a natural talent or calling. It is in the sharing of this gift that you set in motion Universal Law. Known by various names: Cause and Effect, Sowing and Reaping or Karma, this Law governs the experiences you create and the people you attract into your life. When you are in alignment with your Life Purpose you are using the Law to create harmony, peace and prosperity in your life. Live out of sync with your Life Purpose, withhold your special gift, and the Law withholds from you in like measure.

It is through the awareness and proper use of this Law that you harness the awesome Power that is *in* you but not *of* you. With this Power you can rise above any problem, overcome any obstacle and transcend any adversity. The lives of people like Gandhi, Dr. Martin Luther King, Jr., Mother Theresa, Nelson Mandela, etc. should provide sufficient evidence to even the most skeptical that *nothing* is impossible for you when your life is dedicated to a purpose greater than yourself.

Here is my personal experience with the Law:

I did not start out to write a book initially. As a matter of fact, at a time when I was totally frustrated, stressed and aware that I was definitely NOT living my purpose, I began to write down what it would look like to me if I was living the life I was born to live. I simply wrote the first things that came to mind. I initially had about ten. I decided to share my discoveries with some co-workers and friends. Suddenly, I experienced the following phenomena. After I shared, more "secrets" came to mind. I wrote these down and circulated them as well. After I did this, MORE came to mind and the more I shared the more that came to me until my mind was completely flooded and I could scarcely think about anything else. For three days and nights I literally could not sleep as the ideas poured out of me like a huge dam had burst. The Universal Law was put in motion. It was not until I had approached one hundred and had received some positive feedback did I conceive of creating this book. My frustration and stress, once again, served a purpose.

Albert Einstein once said, *"I can't believe that God plays dice with the universe."* If he is right, and I believe he is, then I think it is logical to assume that neither does He play dice with His creations. This book was created to give you some clues to help you tell if you are living your Life Purpose. The quotes were added later for balance and to provide insight. My hope is that by reading this book you will be inspired to *remember* what your soul came to this earth to do and to gain greater confidence that you can accomplish it. The still small Voice inside you will guide you. The rest is up to you.


Peace,

Daniel Ortiz

*Secret #1*

# You know you are living your life purpose if...

*...you are full of energy*
*&*
*void of stress!*

*"Every time you don't follow your inner guidance, you feel a loss of energy, loss of power, a sense of spiritual deadness."*
**-Shakti Gawain**

*"I am never weary of being useful... In serving others I cannot do enough. No labor is sufficient to tire me."*
**-Leonardo Da Vinci**

*Secret #2*

# You know you are living your life purpose if...

*...sleep is an intrusion on your time*
*&*
*not a refuge from your troubles!*

*"Fatigue is often caused not by work, but by worry, frustration and resentment. We rarely get tired when we are doing something interesting and exciting.*

**-Dale Carnegie**

# You know you are living your life purpose if...

*...food & drink
are used to nourish your body
& not to numb your pain!*

*"Never eat more than you can lift."*
**Miss Piggy**

# You know you are living your life purpose if...

*...money is a consequence of your work & not its primary objective!*

*"If money is your hope for independence, you will never have it. The only real security that a man can have in this world is a reserve of knowledge, experience and ability."*
**Henry Ford**

*"We work to become, not to acquire."*
**Elbert Hubbard**

*Secret #5*

# You know you are living your life purpose if...

*...adults think you are crazy*
*&*
*children think you are cool!*

*"We don't like their sound,
and guitar music is on the way out."*
**Decca Recording Co.,
rejecting the Beatles in 1962**

*"Great spirits have always encountered
violent opposition from mediocre minds"*
**Albert Einstein**

# You know you are living your life purpose if...

*...you feel inferior to no one richer*
*&*
*superior to no one poorer!*

*"Measure wealth not by the things you have, but by the things you have for which you would not take money."*
**Author Unknown**

# You know you are living your life purpose if...

*...you feel younger than you look*

*&*

*are wise beyond your years!*

*"How old would you be if you didn't know how old you were?*
**Ruth Gordon**

*"Ah, but I was so much older then, I'm so much younger than that now."*
**Bob Dylan**

# You know you are living your life purpose if...

*...you value
wisdom more than knowledge
& people more than objects!*

*"Keep the gold and keep the silver,
but give us wisdom."*
**Arabian Proverb**

*"We too often love things and use people
when we should be using things
and loving people."*
**Reul L. Howe**

# You know you are living your life purpose if...

*...the past is not a burden*
*&*
*the future of no concern!*

*"You don't understand.
I coulda had class, I coulda been
a contender. I coulda been somebody..."*
**Terry Malloy (Marlon Brando)**
***On The Waterfront***

*"Trust the past to God's mercy,
the present to God's love and
the future to God's providence."*
**St. Augistine**

*Secret #10*

# You know you are living your life purpose if...

*...you are never sick
&
always in the mood!*

*"To follow the Way do not push away anything, even sensual experiences and thoughts. In fact, to accept them completely is enlightenment."*

**Seng-T-'San**

*Secret #11*

# You know you are living your life purpose if...

*...the clothes you wear reflects **your** style & not just what's **in** style!*

*"Your image should be neither contrived nor predictable. When you introduce yourself you want others to be impressed with you, the individual first. The right image is not about expensive clothes or coordinated accessories, it's about being you."*

**Mary Spillane & Christine Sherlock, authors of *Looking Your Best***

*"Clothes make the man. Naked people have little or no influence in society."*

**Mark Twain**

*Secret #12*

# You know you are living your life purpose if...

*...you are patient with the ignorant*
*&*
*tolerate no fool!*

*"If an Aborigine drafted an IQ test, all of Western Civilization would presumabely flunk it."*
**Stanley Garn**

# You know you are living your life purpose if...

*...looking good
is never chosen over
doing right!*

*"You look Maah-velous!*
*It is better to LOOK Maah-velous*
*than to FEEL Maah-velous!"*
**Billy Crystal as *Fernando***

# You know you are living your life purpose if...

*...you give without conditions*
*&*
*receive without guilt!*

*"If we bestow a gift or favor and expect a return for it, it is not a gift but a trade."*
**Anonymous**

# You know you are living your life purpose if...

*...you face your fear
&
express your talent!*

*"Our deepest fear
is not that we are inadequate.
Our deepest fear is that we are
powerful beyond measure.
It is our light, not our darkness,
that most frightens us.
We ask ourselves, who am I to be
brilliant, gorgeous,
talented and fabulous.
Actually, who are you not to be?
You are a child of God.
Your playing small
doesn't serve the world.
There is nothing enlightened
about shrinking so that other people
won't feel insecure around you.
We were born to make manifest
the glory of God that is within us.
It is not just in some of us:
it is in everyone.
And when we let our own light shine,
we unconsciously give other people
permission to do the same.
As we are liberated from our own fear,
our presence automatically
liberates others."*
**Nelson Mandela**

*Secret #16*

# You know you are living your life purpose if...

*...you respect the elderly*
*&*
*question authority!*

*"Pay no attention to that man behind that...ah...er...curtain!*

**Wizard of Oz**

*Secret #17*

# You know you are living your life purpose if...

*...you give back to your community*
*&*
*pamper yourself!*

*"Self-love is not
only necessary and good,
it is a prerequisite for loving others."*
**Rollo May**

*"...And so my fellow Americans
ask not what your country can do for you,
ask what you can do for your country."*
**John F. Kennedy**

# You know you are living your life purpose if...

*...you acknowledge tradition*
*&*
*challenge the status quo!*

*"Every society honors its
live conformists & dead troublemakers."*

**Mignon Malaughlin**

# You know you are living your life purpose if...

*...you are old enough to know better*
*&*
*young enough to do it anyway!*

*"The follies which a person regrets most in life are those he didn't commit when he had the opportunity."*
**Helen Rowland (1876-1950)**

*"Every man dies.*
*Not every man **really** lives."*
**William Wallace (Mel Gibson)**
***Braveheart***

# You know you are living your life purpose if...

*...you lead by example*
*&*
*follow your intuition!*

*"A feeling is not much to go on."*
*"Sometimes a feeling, Mister Spock,
is all we humans have to go on."*
**Spock & Kirk**
***Star Trek***


*"Intuition is everything."*
**Albert Einstein**

# You know you are living your life purpose if...

*...you can love many*
*&*
*remain faithful to one!*

*"The easiest kind of relationship for me is with ten thousand people. The hardest is with one."*
**Joan Baez**

# You know you are living your life purpose if...

*...you know why the life of a Marilyn Monroe could not fill the heart of a Norma Jean!*

*"Resolve to be thyself,
and know that he who finds himself,
loses misery."*
**Coventry Patmore**

# You know you are living your life purpose if...

*...you can win without gloating*
*&*
*lose without anger!*

*"Are you suggesting that
there is some value in losing?"
"Yes. That's the great teacher.
We humans learn more often from
a failure or mistake than we do
from an easy success."*
**Pulaski and Data**
***Star Trek The Next Generation***


*"When you lose,
make sure you don't lose the lesson."*
**Anonymous**

# You know you are living your life purpose if...

*...you can receive a compliment with a simple "thank you" and then shut up!*

*"I'm trying to thank you,
you pointed-ear hobgoblin!"*
*"Oh, yes, you humans have that
emotional need to express gratitude.
'Your welcome,' I believe,
is the correct response."*
**McCoy and Spock**
***Star Trek***

*Secret #25*

# You know you are living your life purpose if...

*...you have the strength
to laugh at yourself &
the sensitivity to cry at movies!*

*"Any man who doesn't cry scares me a little bit."*
**General Norman Schwarzkopf**

# You know you are living your life purpose if...

*...you can influence without speaking
&
teach without credentials!*

*"My life is my teaching."*
**Mahatma Gandhi**

# You know you are living your life purpose if...

*...you can love your enemies*
*&*
*cut yourself some slack!*

*"If I knew the sorrows of
my enemies heart, I could not raise
my sword against him."*
**Ancient Samari Saying**

*"Do not criticize yourself because
in darkness you could not see."*
**Emmanuel**

# You know you are living your life purpose if...

*...you withhold your opinions*
*&*
*give advice reluctantly!*

*"Before you speak, ask yourself,
is it kind, is it necessary, is it true,
does it improve upon the silence?*
**Sai Baba**

*"Everyone is eager to garland my photo,
but no one wants to take my advice."*
**Mahatma Ghandi**

# You know you are living your life purpose if...

*...your sleep is peaceful
& you know what it means to be*
AWAKE!

*"The good people sleep much better
at night than the bad people.
Of course, the bad people enjoy
the waking hours more."*
**Woody Allen**


*"It takes a person who is wide-awake
to make his dreams come true."*
**Robert Babson**

# You know you are living your life purpose if...

*...your curiosity
is never satisfied at the expense
of someone's privacy!*

*"Great minds discuss ideas,
average minds discuss events,
small minds discuss people."*
**Lawrence J. Peter**

# You know you are living your life purpose if...

*...you recognize that anything "New Age" is really old news with bad marketing!*

*"There are no new truths,
but only truths that have
not been recognized."*
**Mary McCarty**

# You know you are living your life purpose if...

*...your worldly ambitions
are in alignment with
the Divine Plan!*

*"I can't believe that God plays dice with the universe."*
**Albert Einstein**

# You know you are living your life purpose if...

*...you sing in the shower*
*&*
*hum while you dress!*

*"Do I sing because I'm happy...Or am I happy because I sing?"*
**Anonymous**

# You know you are living your life purpose if...

*...you see something
good or bad & know that
only your thinking makes it so!*

*"Oh, there's a big difference, Mrs. De Marco. The mob is run by murdering, thieving, lying, cheating, psychopaths. We work for the President of the United States."*
**FBI Director Franklin**
*Married To The Mob*

# You know you are living your life purpose if...

*...you are misunderstood by the masses & unimpressed with the elite!*

*"Is it so bad to be misunderstood?
Pythagoras was misunderstood,
and Socrates, and Jesus, and Luther,
and Copernicus, and Galileo, and
Newton, and every pure and wise spirit
that ever took flesh. To be great is to be
misunderstood."*
**Ralph Waldo Emerson**

*Secret #36*

# You know you are living your life purpose if...

*...you tune in to Oprah*
*&*
*turn off Jerry Springer!*

*"Tell me what you pay attention to and I will tell you who you are."*

**Jose Ortega y Gasset**

# You know you are living your life purpose if...

*...you don't mistake activity with productivity!*

*"Patience is power;
with time and patience,
a mulberry leaf becomes silk."*
**Chinese Proverb**

# You know you are living your life purpose if...

*...you know the difference between knowing the path & walking the path is faith!*

*"What can be gained by
thinking about the scriptures?
What fools! They think themselves
to death with information about the path,
but never take the plunge!"*
**Ramakrishna**

*"Knowing what to do is not enough,
you must do what you know."*
**Anthony Robbins**

# You know you are living your life purpose if...

*...you tell the truth
when you could get away
with a lie!*

*"The only man who is really free
is the one who can turn down
an invitation to dinner without
giving an excuse."*
**Jules Renard**

*"Half the truth is often a great lie."*
**Anonymous**

# You know you are living your life purpose if...

*...you demonstrate the courage to "zig" when everyone else is "zagging!"*

*"The opposite of courage in society is not cowardice; it is conformity."*
**Rollo May**

*"Conformity is the jailer of freedom and the enemy of growth."*
**John F. Kennedy**

# You know you are living your life purpose if...

*...you would rather keep a friend than make a point!*

*"When rejecting the ideas of another, make sure you reject the idea and not the person."*
**Anonymous**

# You know you are living your life purpose if...

*...you don't mistake
a diploma for an education
or a license for expertise!*

*"The concept is interesting and well informed, but in order to earn better than a "C," the idea must be feasible."*
**A Yale University professor
in response to Fred Smith's proposal;
Federal Express**

*"Neither lofty degree of intelligence nor imagination nor both together go into the making of genius. Love, love, love; that is the soul of genius."*
**Wolfgang Amadeus Mozart**

# You know you are living your life purpose if...

*...the difference between you and the rest of the world is that you know in Reality there is no difference!*

*"When indeed, shall we learn that we are all related to one another, that we are all members of one body? Until the spirit of love for our fellow man, regardless of race, color or creed, shall fill the world, making real in our lives and our deeds the actuality of human brotherhood - until the great mass of the people shall be filled with the sense of responsibility for each other's welfare, social justice can never be attained."*

**Helen Keller (1880-1968)**

# You know you are living your life purpose if...

*...you follow your heart*
*&*
*use your head!*

*"If you are doing what you love
and the money has not followed,
chances are good you neglected to
create a business plan first."*
**Daniel Ortiz**

*"Trust Allah,
but tie your camel."*
**The Koran**

# You know you are living your life purpose if...

*...you realize that
success is in your Mind
& fullfillment is of your Spirit!*

*"No matter how grand your vision or big your dream, it is insignificant compared to what you behold when you AWAKEN."*
**Daniel Ortiz**

*"I'd rather be a failure at something I love than a success at something I hate."*
**George Burns**

# You know you are living your life purpose if...

*...you know that true self-esteem comes from knowing your Higher Self!*

*"Your self-confidence will improve when you realize who you are. You are God's child, and capable of acting that way..."*
**Peace Pilgrim**

# You know you are living your life purpose if...

*...you accept that
great achievments are gained
by humble tasks!*

*"We can do no great things-
only small things with great love."*
**Mother Theresa**

# You know you are living your life purpose if...

*...you face your inner demons*
*&*
*speak to your guardian angels!*

*"That which we do not confront in ourselves we will meet as fate."*
**Carl Jung**

*Secret #49*

# You know you are living your life purpose if...

*...you know that in order to reach your highest potential you must first master your lower nature!*

*"No man is free who is not master of himself."*
**Epictetus (A.D. 60-110)**

*Secret #50*

# You know you are living your life purpose if...

*...your outer smile reflects an inner glow!*

*"If there is light in the soul,
there will be beauty in the person."*
**Chinese Proverb**

# You know you are living your life purpose if...

*...you never hurry*
*&*
*are always on time!*

*"So you worry that you are not at the point in your life you should be... Has God shown you a schedule?"*
**Emmanuel**

# You know you are living your life purpose if...

*...you keep your word*
*&*
*let go of grievences!*

*"The 3 hardest tasks in the world
are neither physical feats
nor intellectual achievements,
but moral acts;
to return love for hate,
to include the excluded, and
to say I was wrong."*
**Ernst Heinrich Haeckel**

# You know you are living your life purpose if...

*...you learn more from watching children at play than from adults at work!*

*"All I really need to know about
how to live and what to do and
how to be I learned in kindergarden.
Wisdom was not at the top of the
graduate-school mountain, but
there in the sandpile at Sunday school."*
**Robert Fulghum**

# You know you are living your life purpose if...

*...your treatment of others reflects not their station in life but yours!*

*"This is the final test of a gentleman;*
*his respect for those who can be*
*of no possible service to him."*
**William Lyon Phelps (1865-1943)**

*"Be kind, for everyone you meet*
*is fighting a hard battle."*
**Plato (427-347 B.C.)**

# You know you are living your life purpose if...

*...you look outside to dream*
*&*
*within to Awaken!*

*"Once upon a time I dreamed that I was a butterfly...Suddenly I awakened and there I lay, myself again. Now I do not know whether I was then a man dreaming I was a butterfly, or whether I am now a butterfly dreaming I am a man."*
**Chuang-Tzu (3rd Century B.C.)**

# You know you are living your life purpose if...

*...you know
the secret to being rich
is to be content with what you have!*

*"The real measure of our wealth is our worth if we lost our money."*
**Anonymous**

# You know you are living your life purpose if...

*...you know the secret
to enjoying life is not having more
but wanting less!*

*"Those who want much,
are always much in need."*
**Horace (65-8 B.C.)**

# You know you are living your life purpose if...

*...you know that*
*if it is religious it is cultural &*
*if it is spiritual it is universal!*

*"Truth is One
and the learned call it
by many names."*
**Rig Veda**

*"A universal theology is impossible,
but a universal experience is not only
possible but necessary."*
**A Course In Miracles**

# You know you are living your life purpose if...

*...you know that
no matter how strong your will,
there is One that is greater!*

*"I am a Klingon warrior and a Starfleet officer. I have piloted starships through Dominion mine fields, I have stood in battle against Kelvans twice my size, I courted and won the heart of the magnificent Jadzia Dax. If I can do those things...I can make this child go to sleep!"*

**Worf to Dax, on babysitting Kirayoshi**
*Star Trek Deep Space 9*

*Secret* #60

# You know you are living your life purpose if...

*...when you want to know
what to do with your life,
you ask yourself
what you love to do with your time!*

*"Let the beauty we love
be what we do."*
**Rumi**

# You know you are living your life purpose if...

*...you know that to learn the ways of Heaven you need only unlearn the ways of the world!*

*"The words of Truth
are always paradoxical."*
**Lao Tzu**

# You know you are living your life purpose if...

*...you realize that
your body cannot enter Heaven
& your spirit never left it!*

*"When your body and your ego and your dreams are gone, you will know that you will last forever."*
**A Course In Miracles**

# You know you are living your life purpose if...

*...you know
the true purpose of prosperity
is not to inflate your ego but
to enrich your soul!*

*"Now mama said there's only
so much fortune a man really needs
and the rest is just for showing off."*
**Forest Gump (Tom Hanks)**
*Forest Gump*

*"Many of the luxuries and many
so-called comforts of life are not only
indispensible, but positive hinderences
to the elevation of mankind."*
**Henry David Thoreau**

# You know you are living your life purpose if...

*...you know that
in order to perceive Reality
you must first recognize that
the world is an illusion!*

*"All the world's a stage,
And all the men and women merely players.
They have their exits and their entrances,
And one man in his time plays many parts."*
**William Shakespeare**

# You know you are living your life purpose if...

*...you know that to see the face of God you need only look into the eyes of your neighbor!*

*"I sought my soul,
but my soul I could not see,
I sought my God but He eluded me,
I sought my brother and I found all three."*
**A young civil rights advocate**

# You know you are living your life purpose if...

*...you finally realize that your will & God's Will have one thing in common: They are the same!*

*"You are afraid of God's Will,
because you believe it is not yours.
This belief is your whole sickness and
fear arises here, because this is the
belief that makes you* want *not to know.
Believing this you hide in darkness,
denying that the light is in you."*
**A Course In Miracles**

# You know you are living your life purpose if...

*...you don't fear the devil because you know the devil is fear!*

*"It is one of the great jokes of existence.
When people have the courage to
journey into the center of their fear,
they find - nothing.
The terror was only layers of fear
being afraid of itself."*
**Peter McWilliams**


*"The only thing to fear...is fear itself."*
**Franklin Delano Roosevelt**

# You know you are living your life purpose if...

*...you realize that what you really want from life is something to give it!*

*"You were born to create."*

**A Course In Miracles**

# You know you are living your life purpose if...

*...you realize that
what you really want from others
is to give them a part of yourself!*

*"You give but little when you give of your possessions. It is when you give of yourself that you truly give."*
**Kahlil Gibran**

# You know you are living your life purpose if...

*...the power of your mind
serves the wisdom
of your heart!*

*"It is not enough to have a good mind;
the main thing is to use it well."*
**Rene Descartes**

# You know you are living your life purpose if...

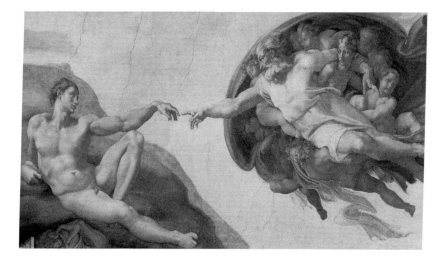

*...you know that
in order to save the world
you need only heal your soul!*

*"When the soul cries out,
it is a sign that we have arrived at
a necessary stage of self-reflection.
The secret is not to get stuck there
dithering or wringing your hands,
but to move forward by resolution to
heal **yourself.***
**Epictetus (A.D. 55-135)**

*"The broken become expert at mending."*
**Anonymous**

# You know you are living your life purpose if...

*...you see God as
the Creator in Heaven
& not a sugardaddy in the sky!*

*"It is all too possible to want gifts from the Lord, but not the Lord Himself - which is to imply that the gift is preferable to the giver."*
**St. Augustine**

*"When the gods want to punish you, they answer your prayers."*
**Anonymous**

# You know you are living your life purpose if...

*...you know that
what you pursue will elude you &
what you become you will attract!*

*"Don't aim at success;*
*the more you aim at it and make it*
*a target, the more you are going to miss it.*
*For success, like happiness,*
*cannot be pursued. It must ensue...*
*as the unintended side-effect of*
*one's personal dedication to a course*
*greater than oneself."*
**Victor Frankl**

# You know you are living your life purpose if...

*...you know that we are not physical bodies trying to get to Heaven but are spiritual beings who forgot it!*

*"When you find the light within you,
you will realize it has always been there."*
**Emmanuel**

# You know you are living your life purpose if...

*...you know that
the quickest way to find God
is to want nothing else!*

*"If you want Truth*
*as badly as a drowning man wants air,*
*you will realize it in a split second."*
**The Upanishads**

# You know you are living your life purpose if...

*...you have been humbled in the past*
*&*
*have become greater as a result!*

*"The deeper that sorrow
carves into your being, the more joy
you can contain...When you are joyous,
look deep into your heart and you shall
find it is only that which has given you
sorrow that is giving you joy."*
**Kahlil Gibran**

*"Failure is nature's plan
to prepare you for great responsibilities."*
**Napoleon Hill**

# You know you are living your life purpose if...

*...you can think
not only "outside the box"
but also Above it!*

*"And now here is my secret,
a very simple secret;
it is only with the heart
that one can see rightly, what is essential
is invisible to the eye."*
**Antoine de Saint-Exupery**

# You know you are living your life purpose if...

*...you see the glass as neither half full nor half empty but as a reflection of yourself!*

*"We do not see things as they are.*
*We see them as we are."*
**The Talmud**

# You know you are living your life purpose if...

*...you know that to hear the voice of God you need only listen to the sound of silence!*

*"I found I had less and less to say, until I became silent, and began to listen. I discovered in the silence, the voice of God."*
**Soren Kierkegaard**

# You know you are living your life purpose if...

*...you know that
in order to understand Truth
you must first let go of
what you **believe** is true!*

*"Don't search for Truth.
Just stop having opinions."*
**Seng-T' San**

*The Three Stages Of A Man's Life:
1. He believes in Santa Claus
2. He doesn't believe in Santa Claus
3. He is Santa Claus*
**Anonymous**

# You know you are living your life purpose if...

*...you realize that the purpose of this world is not to arrive at a destination or to experience the journey but to accelerate your* AWAKENING!

*"Forget not that the healing of
God's Son is all the world is for."*
**A Course In Miracles**

*"You are not here to change the world,
the world is here to change you."*
**Shantidasa**

# You know you are living your life purpose if...

*...you see no difference between the poor man who has not the means to afford a fine meal and the rich man who has not the appetite to enjoy it!*

*"The demands, and consequently the needs, are the same or very similar, no matter where we are in the world. In spite of everything, I think that in the West, in general, the needs are mostly spiritual. Material needs, in most cases, are taken care of. Rather, there is an immense spiritual poverty."*
**Mother Theresa**

*"There are two tragedies in life. One is not to get your hearts desire. The other is to get it."*
**George Bernard Shaw**

# You know you are living your life purpose if...

*...you know that less can be more*
*&*
*being at the top can be a let down!*

*"Disillusion; Climbing to the top
of the ladder of success and finding
you have leaned it against the wrong wall."*
**Colin Bowles**

# You know you are living your life purpose if...

*...you know the secret to happiness is not found by gaining what you desire but in detaching yourself from the desire!*

*"After a time,
you may find that "having" is
not so pleasing a thing, after all,
as "wanting." It is not logical,
but it is often true."*

**Spock**

***Star Trek***

*"Show me the fruit of your desires
and I will show you the seed
of your suffering."*

**Daniel Ortiz**

# You know you are living your life purpose if...

*...you know that*
*your possessions can possess you,*
*your desires can torment you*
*& releasing both can free you!*

*"He who is not content with what he has, would not be content with what he would like to have."*
**Socrates (470 - 399 B.C.)**

# You know you are living your life purpose if...

*...you spend time with family & money with caution!*

*"If you bungle raising your children,
I don't think whatever else you do
matters very much."*
**Jacqueline Kennedy Onassis**

*Secret #87*

# You know you are living your life purpose if...

*...you know that
most fear death, some fear life,
few fear nothing & all fear illusions!*

*"Your greatest gift
lies beyond the door named fear."*
**Sufi Saying**

# You know you are living your life purpose if...

*...when you are not doing what you love, you do what you do* **with** *love!*

*"I long to accomplish a great and noble task, but it is my duty to accomplish small tasks as if they were great and noble."*
**Helen Keller (1880 -1968)**

# You know you are living your life purpose if...

*...you know that*
*the great are served by the humble*
*& the humble are served*
*only by the truly great!*

*"Someone once told me that
not even for a million dollars
would they touch a leper. I responded:
"Neither would I. If it were a case of money,
I would not even do it for two million.
On the other hand, I do it gladly for
the love of God."*
**Mother Theresa**

# You know you are living your life purpose if...

*...you know that*
*in order to Have it all*
*you need only Be who you are*
*& Do what you love!*

*"The truth is that all of us attain the greatest success and happiness possible in this life whenever we use our native capacities to their greatest extent."*
**Dr. Smiley Blanton**

*"A musician must make music, an artist must paint, a poet must write if he is ultimately to be at peace with himself."*
**Abraham Maslow**

# You know you are living your life purpose if...

*..you know that the true measure of wealth is not how much you can afford to spend, but how much you can afford to give away!*

*"A man's wealth is
the good he does in the world."*
**Muhammad**

# You know you are living your life purpose if...

*...your heart is full,
your mind is tamed
and your soul is liberated!*

*"When we let freedom ring,*
*when we let it ring from every village*
*and every hamlet, from every state*
*and every city, we will be able to*
*speed up that day when*
*all of God's children,*
*black men and white men,*
*Jews and Gentiles,*
*Protestants and Catholics,*
*will be able to join hands and sing*
*in the words of that old Negro spiritual,*
*"Free at last! Free at last!*
*Thank God Almighty,*
*we are free at last!"*
**Dr. Martin Luther King, Jr.**

# You know you are living your life purpose if...

*...you know this world is neither Heaven nor Hell but can reflect each!*

*"It is possible for one person
to be living in heaven and for
another to be living in hell and both
be living under the same roof."*
**Anonymous**

*"The mind is its own place,
and in itself can make a
heaven of Hell, a hell of Heaven."*
**John Milton**

# You know you are living your life purpose if...

*...you know that
your body can betray you,
your mind can deceive you &
your Spirit will never leave you!*

*"The kingdom of God is within you."*
**Jesus**

# You know you are living your life purpose if...

*...you know that
when you serve others
it is your Self who benefits!*

*"If you want happiness for an hour -
take a nap.
If you want happiness for a day -
go fishing.
If you want happiness for a month -
get married.
If you want happiness for a year -
inherit a fortune.
If you want happiness for life -
help others."*
**Chinese Proverb**

# You know you are living your life purpose if...

*...you know that
the best way to end your suffering
is to end the suffering of others!*

*"Our brothers' needs become our own, because they are taking the journey with us as we go to God. Without us they would lose their way. Without them we could never find our own."*

**A Course In Miracles**

*Secret #97*

# You know you are living your life purpose if...

*...you are consistent in thought, word & deed!*

*"Watch your thoughts;*
*they become words.*
*Watch your words;*
*they become actions.*
*Watch your actions;*
*they become habits.*
*Watch your habits;*
*they become character.*
*Watch your character;*
*it becomes your destiny.*
**Frank Outlaw**

# You know you are living your life purpose if...

*...what you do for a living is a reflection of who you are & not just what you want!*

*"The biggest mistake people make in life is not trying to make a living doing what they most enjoy."*

**Malcomb Forbes**

*"Where your talents and the need of the world cross, there lies your vocation."*

**Aristotle**

*Secret #99*

# You know you are living your life purpose if...

*...you know that whether you feel rich or poor, blessed or cursed, depends on whom you compare yourself to!*

*"I cried because I had no shoes until I met a man who had no feet."*
**Persian saying**

# You know you are living your life purpose if...

*...you experience synchronicity
& know that there is no such thing
as coincidence!*

*Synchronicity:*
*"A meaningful coincidence*
*of two or more events where something*
*other than the probability of chance*
*is involved."*
**Carl Jung**

# You know you are living your life purpose if...

*...you fear nothing*
*&*
*know that love is all that matters!*

*"The conclusion is always the same;
Love is the most powerful and still the
most unknown energy in the world."*
**Teilhard de Chardin**

*"And that's the way it is."*
**Walter Cronkite**

*You have a purpose only as long as you are not complete; until then, completeness, perfection, is the purpose.*
- Nisargatta

*Those who have failed to work toward the truth have missed the purpose of living.*
- Buddha

*Learn to get in touch with silence within yourself and know that everything in this life has a purpose.*
- Elizabeth Kubler-Ross

*The purpose of life is to unlearn what has been learned and to remember what has been forgotten.*
- Sufi saying

*The possibilities are unlimited as long as you are true to your life's purpose.*
- Marcia Wieder

*What allows us, as human beings, to psychologically survive life on earth, with all of its pain, drama, and challenges, is a sense of purpose and meaning.*
- Barbara De Angelis

*You will All come to the ultimate wisdom of your true Selves. It is inevitable. That is the purpose of your journey.*
- Emmanuel

*It is a paradox of life that the way to miss pleasure is to seek it first. The very first condition of lasting happiness is that life should be full of purpose, aiming at something outside self.*
- Hugo C. Black

*Awake and remember your purpose, for it is your will to do so.*
- A Course In Miracles

*This is true joy of life - the being used for a purpose that is recognized by yourself as the right one...*
- George Bernard Shaw

*What our deepest self craves is not mere enjoyment, but some supreme purpose that will enlist all our powers and give unity and direction to our life.*
- Henry J. Golding

*When you begin to think and grow rich, you will observe that riches begin with a state of mind, with definiteness of purpose, with little or no hard work.*
- Napoleon Hill

*The purpose of life...is to live it, to taste experience to the utmost, to reach out eagerly and without fear for newer and richer experience.*
- Eleanor Roosevelt

*I don't think any of us really KNOWS why we're here. But I think we're supposed to BELIEVE we're here for a purpose.*
- Ray Charles

*There is only one purpose for all life, and that is for you and all that lives to experience fullest glory.*
- Neale Donald Walsch
Author: *Conversations with God*

*We are all designed for a specific purpose; we all have something for which each of us, and each of us alone, is responsible.*
- Naomi Stephan

*Happines is the meaning and the purpose of life, the whole aim and end of human existence.*
- Aristotle

*The first principle of ethical power is Purpose. By purpose, I don't mean your objective or intention - something toward which you are striving.Purpose is something bigger. It is the picture you have of yourself -the kind of person you want to be.*
-Kenneth Blanchard

*Great minds have purposes; others have wishes.*
- Washington Irving

*No pleasure philosophy, no sensuality, no place nor power, no material success can for a moment give such inner satisfaction as the sense of living for good purpose.*
- Minot Simons

*What men want is not talent; it is purpose; in other words, not the power to achieve, but the will to labor.*
- Edward Bulwer-Lytton

*Divine purpose for us is learning to live in harmony with God's will...When you know your part in the scheme of things, in the Divine Plan, there is never a feeling of inadequacy. You are always given the resources for any situation, any obstacle. There is no strain; there is always security.*
- Peace Pilgrim

*The purpose of human life is to serve...*
- Albert Schweitzer

$1 of every book purchased will be donated to:

**BOYS & GIRLS CLUB**
OF SANTA FE

*The **Positive** Place For Kids*